JEHOVAH PRAYERS
FOR CHILDREN

By Angela Heron

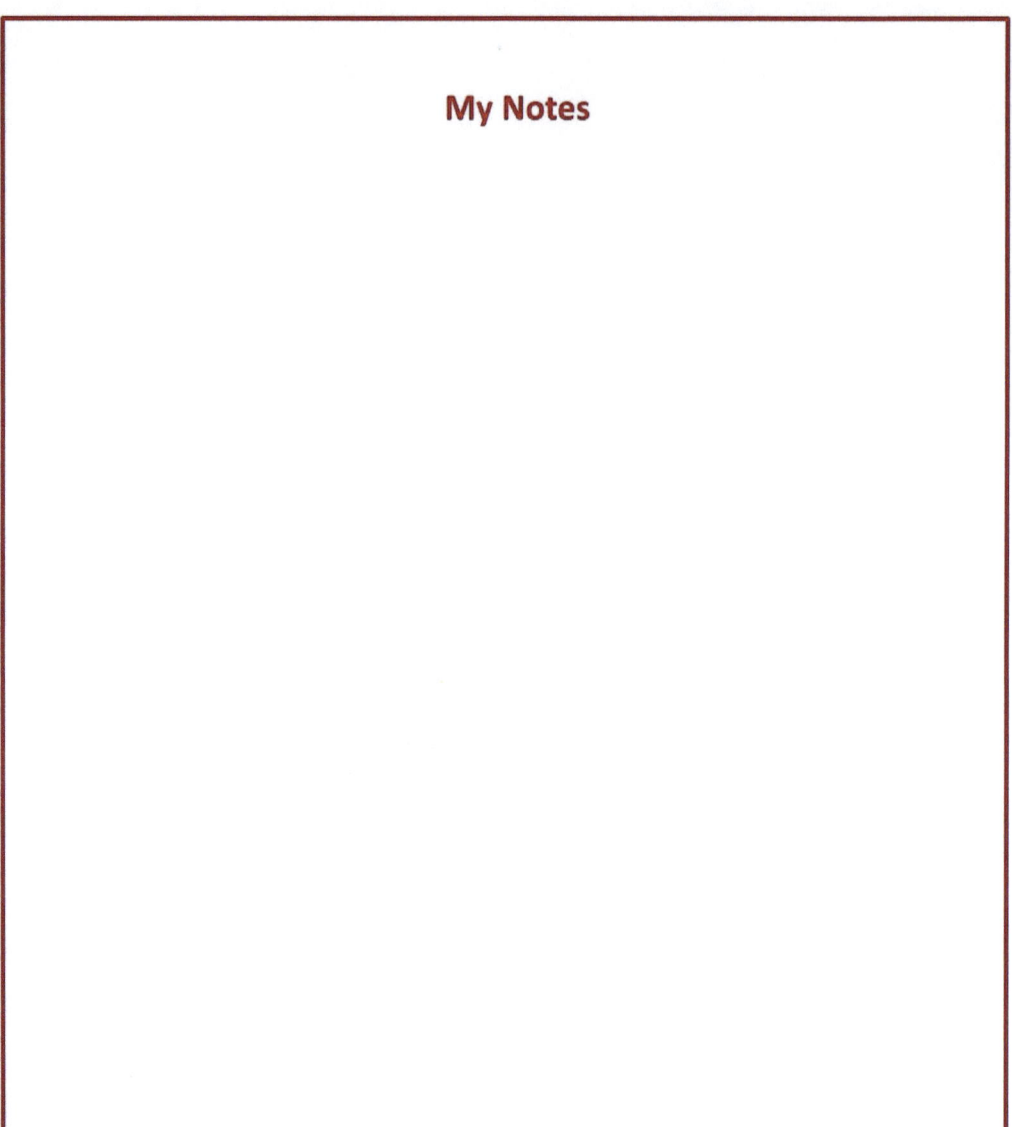

My Notes

Jehovah Prayers
FOR CHILDREN

Copyright © 2016 Angela Heron. All rights reserved.
First paperback edition printed 2016 in the United Kingdom
A catalogue record for this book is available from the British Library.
ISBN **978-1-5262-0090-7**

No part of this book shall be reproduced or transmitted in any form or by any means, electronic or mechanical, including photocopying, recording, or by any information retrieval system without written permission of the publisher.

Published by Jehovah Blessings Publishing.
For more copies of this book, please email:
info@jehovahblessings.co.uk
Printed in Great Britain.

JEHOVAH PRAYERS

Prayers are for all times – even to give thanks for all the good things that God has done and is still doing for us every day.

God cares for you in so many ways. His different names show who He is as He provides for all our needs. Turn to Him today and pray.

Rejoice always, pray without ceasing, in everything give thanks; for this is the will of God in Christ Jesus. **1 Thessalonians 5:16-18**

All scripture quotations, unless otherwise stated, are taken from the *New King James version*.

JEHOVA ELOHIM

The Eternal Creator

Thank You for everything on this earth that You created God!

JEHOVA ELOHIM

The Creator of everything in heaven and on earth.
Ephesians 3:15

The Eternal Creator

JEHOVA ELOHIM

Genesis 1:27
You were created in God's image.

The Eternal Creator

You can write your own prayer here.

JEHOVA ELOHIM

The Eternal Creator

Has God answered your prayer?

JEHOVA ELOHIM

The Eternal Creator

You can write your own prayer here.

JEHOVA ELOHIM

The Eternal Creator

You can write your own prayer here.

JEHOVA ELOHIM

The Eternal Creator

Has God answered your prayer?

JEHOVA ELOHIM

The Eternal Creator

You can write your own prayer here.

JEHOVA ELOHIM

The Eternal Creator

You can write your own prayer here.

JEHOVA ELOHIM

The Eternal Creator

Has God answered your prayer?

JEHOVA ELOHIM

The Eternal Creator

You can write your own prayer here.

JEHOVA ELOHIM

The Eternal Creator

Has God answered your prayer?

JEHOVAH RAPHA

The Lord heals

Thank You God for keeping me well

JEHOVAH RAPHA

Heal me O LORD and I shall be healed.

Jeremiah 17:14

EHOVAH RAPHA

God can make you well.
Exodus 15:26

You can write your own prayer here.

JEHOVAH RAPHA

The Lord heals

Has God answered your prayer?

JEHOVAH RAPHA

The Lord heals

You can write your own prayer here.

JEHOVAH RAPHA

The Lord heals

You can write your own prayer here.

JEHOVAH RAPHA

The Lord heals

24 Has God answered your prayer?

JEHOVAH RAPHA

The Lord heals

You can write your own prayer here.

JEHOVAH RAPHA

The Lord heals

You can write your own prayer here.

JEHOVAH RAPHA

The Lord heals

Has God answered your prayer?

JEHOVAH RAPHA

The Lord heals

You can write your own prayer here.

JEHOVAH RAPHA

The Lord heals

Has God answered your prayer?

The Lord is my Shepherd

JEHOVAH ROHI

"Dear GOD, I thank You for leading me, and guiding me in all the right places."

JEHOVAH ROHI

Seek His will in all you do, and He will show you which path to take.
                                    Proverbs 3:6

JEHOVAH ROHI

Revelation 7:17
The Lord Himself will lead you.

You can write your own prayer here.

JEHOVAH ROHI

The Lord is my Shepherd

Has God answered your prayer?

JEHOVAH ROHI

The Lord is my Shepherd

You can write your own prayer here.

JEHOVAH ROHI

The Lord is my Shepherd

You can write your own prayer here.

JEHOVAH ROHI

The Lord is my Shepherd

Has God answered your prayer?

JEHOVAH ROHI

The Lord is my Shepherd

37   You can write your own prayer here.

JEHOVAH ROHI

The Lord is my Shepherd

38   You can write your own prayer here.

JEHOVAH ROHI

The Lord is my Shepherd

Has God answered your prayer?

JEHOVAH ROHI

The Lord is my Shepherd

You can write your own prayer here.

JEHOVAH ROHI

The Lord is my Shepherd

Has God answered your prayer?

JEHOVAH JIREH — *My Provider*

"I thank You God for every good thing."

JEHOVAH JIREH   *My Provider*

And this same God who takes care of me will supply all your needs from his glorious riches, which have been given to us in Christ Jesus.

Philippians 4:19

JEHOVAH JIREH *My Provider*

God will see to all your needs.
Acts 17:25

You can write your own prayer here.

JEHOVAH JIREH *My Provider*

Has God answered your prayer?

JEHOVAH JIREH   *My Provider*

You can write your own prayer here.

JEHOVAH JIREH *My Provider*

You can write your own prayer here.

Jehovah Jireh

My Provider

Has God answered your prayer?

JEHOVAH JIREH — *My Provider*

You can write your own prayer here.

JEHOVAH JIREH — *My Provider*

You can write your own prayer here.

JEHOVAH JIREH *My Provider*

Has God answered your prayer?

JEHOVAH JIREH *My Provider*

You can write your own prayer here.

JEHOVAH JIREH *My Provider*

Has God answered your prayer?

JEHOVAH SHAMMAH

The Lord is present

Dear GOD, thank You for always being here for me. Your dear child,

----

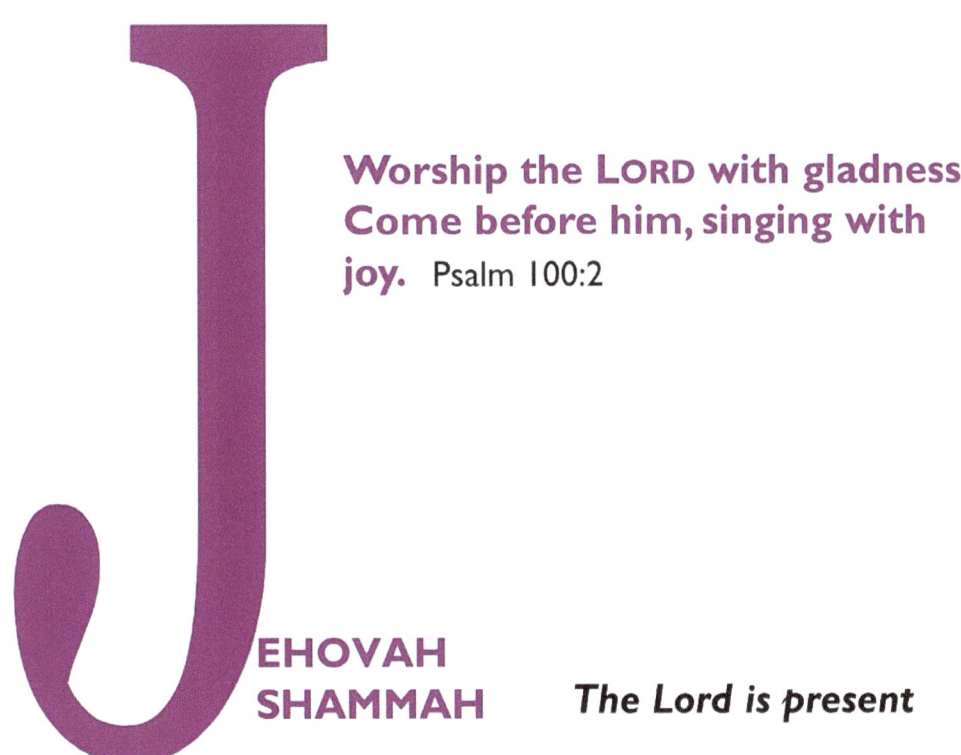

Worship the LORD with gladness. Come before him, singing with joy. Psalm 100:2

JEHOVAH SHAMMAH   *The Lord is present*

JEHOVAH SHAMMAH

You can be near God too.

Psalm 145:18

The Lord is present

You can write your own prayer here.

JEHOVAH SHAMMAH

The Lord is present

Has God answered your prayer?

JEHOVAH SHAMMAH   *The Lord is present*

You can write your own prayer here.

JEHOVAH SHAMMAH   *The Lord is present*

You can write your own prayer here.

JEHOVAH SHAMMAH *The Lord is present*

Has God answered your prayer?

JEHOVAH SHAMMAH *The Lord is present*

You can write your own prayer here.

JEHOVAH SHAMMAH *The Lord is present*

You can write your own prayer here.

JEHOVAH SHAMMAH   *The Lord is present*

Has God answered your prayer?

JEHOVAH SHAMMAH

The Lord is present

You can write your own prayer here.

JEHOVAH SHAMMAH — ***The Lord is present***

Has God answered your prayer?

The Lord our Banner

JEHOVAH NISSI

I thank You Lord that with Your help, I can do all things.

The Lord our Banner

EHOVAH NISSI

Exodus 17:15

Moses built an altar there and named it Yahweh-Nissi (which means "the Lord is my banner").

The Lord our Banner

EHOVAH NISSI

The Lord will lift you up.

Psalm 147:6

You can write your own prayer here.

The Lord our Banner

JEHOVAH NISSI

Has God answered your prayer?

The Lord our Banner

EHOVAH NISSI

You can write your own prayer here.

The Lord our Banner

EHOVAH NISSI

You can write your own prayer here.

The Lord our Banner

EHOVAH NISSI

Has God answered your prayer?

The Lord our Banner

JEHOVAH NISSI

You can write your own prayer here.

The Lord our Banner

EHOVAH NISSI

You can write your own prayer here.

The Lord our Banner

JEHOVAH NISSI

Has God answered your prayer?

The Lord our Banner

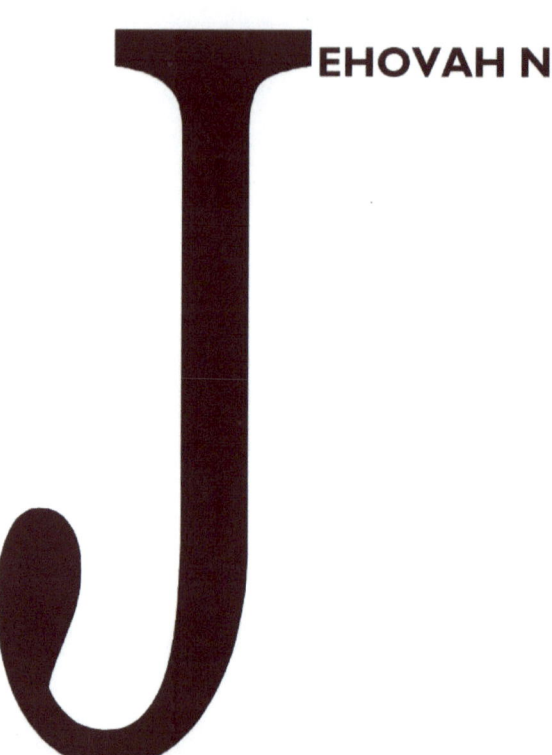EHOVAH NISSI

You can write your own prayer here.

The Lord our Banner

JEHOVAH NISSI

Has God answered your prayer?

The Lord is Peace

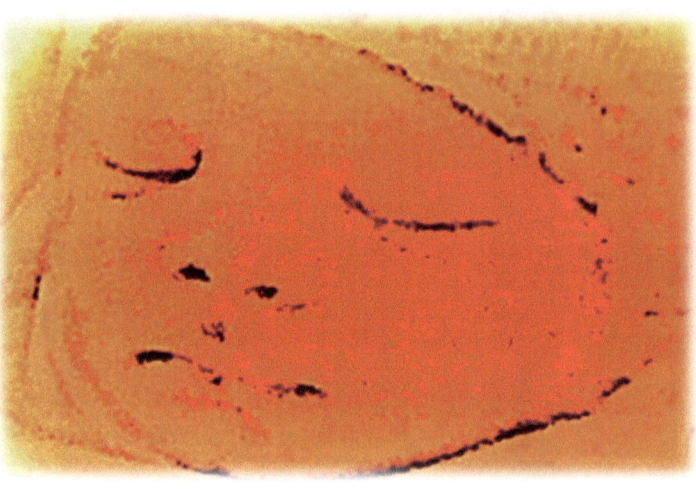

JEHOVAH SHALOM

I thank You God that You are my peace,
You make 'all' things well.

The Lord is Peace

In peace I will lie down and sleep,
for you alone, **O LORD**, will keep me safe.

Psalm 4:8

JEHOVAH SHALOM

The Lord is Peace

JEHOVAH SHALOM   **Peace can be yours.**

Jude 1:2

You can write your own prayer here.

JEHOVAH SHALOM

The Lord is Peace

Has God answered your prayer?

The Lord is Peace

JEHOVAH SHALOM

You can write your own prayer here.

The Lord is Peace

JEHOVAH SHALOM

You can write your own prayer here.

JEHOVAH SHALOM

The Lord is Peace

Has God answered your prayer?

The Lord is Peace

JEHOVAH SHALOM

You can write your own prayer here.

The Lord is Peace

JEHOVAH SHALOM

You can write your own prayer here.

JEHOVAH SHALOM

The Lord is Peace

Has God answered your prayer?

JEHOVAH SHALOM

The Lord is Peace

You can write your own prayer here.

The Lord is Peace

JEHOVAH SHALOM

Has God answered your prayer?

The Lord of Hosts

JEHOVAH SABAOTH

Thank You Lord that You are Lord over all.

The Lord of Hosts

> They were calling out to each other, "Holy, holy, holy is the LORD of Heaven's Armies! The whole earth is filled with his glory!"
>
> Isaiah 6:3

JEHOVAH SABAOTH

The Lord of Hosts

J

The Lord of Hosts will be with you.

Psalm 46:7

EHOVAH SABAOTH

You can write your own prayer here.

The Lord of Hosts

JEHOVAH SABAOTH

Has God answered your prayer?

The Lord of Hosts

JEHOVAH SABAOTH

You can write your own prayer here.

The Lord of Hosts

JEHOVAH SABAOTH

You can write your own prayer here.

The Lord of Hosts

JEHOVAH SABAOTH

Has God answered your prayer?

The Lord of Hosts

JEHOVAH SABAOTH

You can write your own prayer here.

The Lord of Hosts

JEHOVAH SABAOTH

You can write your own prayer here.

The Lord of Hosts

JEHOVAH SABAOTH

Has God answered your prayer?

The Lord of Hosts

JEHOVAH SABAOTH

You can write your own prayer here.

The Lord of Hosts

JEHOVAH SABAOTH

Has God answered your prayer?

Lord I thank You for everything that You have made.

JEHOVAH HOSEENU *The Lord our Maker*

Psalm 95:6
Come, let us worship and bow down.
Let us kneel before the LORD our maker.

JEHOVAH HOSEENU *The Lord our Maker*

J

Do you know the Lord your maker?

Psalm 95:6

JEHOVAH HOSEENU *The Lord our Maker*

You can write your own prayer here.

JEHOVAH HOSEENU *The Lord our Maker*

Has God answered your prayer?

JEHOVAH HOSEENU *The Lord our Maker*

You can write your own prayer here.

JEHOVAH HOSEENU *The Lord our Maker*

You can write your own prayer here.

JEHOVAH HOSEENU *The Lord our Maker*

Has God answered your prayer?

JEHOVAH HOSEENU *The Lord our Maker*

You can write your own prayer here.

JEHOVAH HOSEENU *The Lord our Maker*

You can write your own prayer here.

JEHOVAH HOSEENU *The Lord our Maker*

Has God answered your prayer?

JEHOVAH HOSEENU *The Lord our Maker*

112   You can write your own prayer here.

JEHOVAH HOSEENU *The Lord our Maker*

Has God answered your prayer?

JEHOVAH ELYON

The Lord Most High

There is 'no-one' or 'nothing' higher than You Lord. You are the greatest!

JEHOVAH ELYON

The Lord Most High

I will thank the L ORD because he is just; I will sing praise to the name of the L ORD Most High.   Psalm 7:17

JEHOVAH ELYON

The Lord Most High

Psalm 83:18

Do you know the Lord Most High?

You can write your own prayer here.

JEHOVAH ELYON

The Lord Most High

Has God answered your prayer?

Jehovah Elyon

The Lord Most High

You can write your own prayer here.

JEHOVAH ELYON

The Lord Most High

You can write your own prayer here.

JEHOVAH ELYON

The Lord Most High

Has God answered your prayer?

JEHOVAH ELYON

The Lord Most High

You can write your own prayer here.

JEHOVAH ELYON

The Lord Most High

You can write your own prayer here.

JEHOVAH ELYON

The Lord Most High

Has God answered your prayer?

JEHOVAH ELYON

The Lord Most High

You can write your own prayer here.

JEHOVAH ELYON

The Lord Most High

Has God answered your prayer?

JEHOVAH PRAYERS
FOR CHILDREN

Matthew 19:14 (NLT)

"Let the children come to me. Don't stop them! For the Kingdom of Heaven belongs to those who are like these children"

Teaching our children about the power of prayer will both strengthen their faith & their walk with God. Help your child to know God and be blessed today.

Connect with Jehovah Blessings at:
info@jehovahblessings.co.uk

My Notes

My Notes

My Notes

My Notes

My Notes

www.ingramcontent.com/pod-product-compliance
Lightning Source LLC
Chambersburg PA
CBHW042016150426
43197CB00002B/41